NAMIBIA 2016 HUMAN RIGHTS REPORT

EXECUTIVE SUMMARY

Namibia is a constitutional multiparty democracy. In local and regional elections held in November 2015, the ruling Swapo party won 112 of 121 regional council seats and gained control of 54 of 57 local authorities. Elections held in November 2014 resulted in the election of Prime Minister Hage Geingob to the presidency and retention by Swapo of its large parliamentary majority. International observers characterized the elections in 2014 and 2015 as generally free and fair.

Civilian authorities generally maintained effective control over the security forces.

The most significant human rights problems in the country included the slow pace of judicial proceedings and resulting lengthy pretrial detention, sometimes under poor conditions; violence and discrimination against women and children, including rape; and child labor.

Other governmental human rights problems included corruption by officials, discrimination against ethnic minorities and indigenous people, lack of public access to government information, and attempts to curb media freedom.

The government took steps to prosecute or punish officials who committed abuses, whether in the security services or elsewhere in the government, but impunity existed.

Section 1. Respect for the Integrity of the Person, Including Freedom from:

a. Arbitrary Deprivation of Life and other Unlawful or Politically Motivated Killings

There were no reports the government or its agents committed or were responsible for arbitrary or unlawful killings.

b. Disappearance

There were no reports of politically motivated disappearances.

c. Torture and Other Cruel, Inhuman, or Degrading Treatment or Punishment

The constitution and law prohibit such practices, but the law does not define "torture" or separately classify it as a crime. Torture is prosecuted under criminal provisions such as assault or homicide. The Ombudsman's Office received no complaints of torture by police during the year. April 2015 criminal and civil cases regarding an alleged incident of police torture were pending as of November 2.

Prison and Detention Center Conditions

Prison conditions improved during the year, although some prison buildings remained dilapidated.

Physical Conditions: Conditions in detention centers and police holding cells remained poor. Conditions were often worse in pretrial holding cells than in prisons. Human rights bodies and government officials reported overcrowding in holding cells. Nationwide, police holding cells built to confine 3,523 detainees held an average of 3,676 detainees during the period between April 2014 and March 2015. By March the government built enough additional holding cells so that the nationwide holding cell capacity of 4,066 surpassed the 3,649 inmates incarcerated. Overcrowding, however, remained a problem in six of the country's 14 regions due to insufficient capacity. For example, in Kunene Region the number of detainees in police holding cells was 2.13 times the cells' capacity. In Oshikoto Region the number was 2.06 times capacity. In Khomas Region, which includes the capital and is the most populous region, overcrowding was 1.34 times capacity. Ombudsman's Office staff made regular visits to holding cells to assess their condition.

In pretrial holding cells, sanitation remained insufficient, tuberculosis was prevalent, and on-site nursing was inadequate.

Overcrowding was less of a problem in prisons. As of July prisons built to confine a maximum of 5,147 persons held 3,742 inmates. These included 108 women and eight juveniles. There was overcrowding in only three of the country's 13 prisons--those in Oluno, Omaruru, and Grootfontein.

Prison and holding cell conditions for women were generally better than for men. The Windhoek-based Legal Assistance Center (LAC), a nongovernmental organization (NGO), reported female prisoners could keep their babies with them until age two, and received food and clothing for them from prison staff.

There were limited programs to prevent HIV transmission in prisons. The government refused to distribute condoms to prisoners.

The law does not permit holding juvenile offenders with adults. Prison authorities reported they largely observed the law, but police occasionally held juveniles with adults in rural detention facilities because of a lack of pretrial detainee facilities for juveniles.

Administration: The Ombudsman's Office, an independent authority, investigated credible allegations of inhuman conditions, and reported close cooperation with police in resolving complaints and respond promptly to inquiries. Detainees in the Caprivi treason trial of persons allegedly involved in a 1999 attempt to secede from the country (see section 1.e.) sued the government during their incarceration for assault and deprivation of medical treatment following their arrest in 1999. The LAC represented the majority of the defendants and settled all of the remaining cases by the end of 2015. Civil lawsuits filed by nine acquitted defendants alleging a total of 217 million Namibian dollars (N$) ($15.5 million) in damages began in November. Twenty other acquitted defendants also filed civil lawsuits claiming a combined total of N$302 million ($21.6 million) in damages. On October 24, the prosecutor general moved for a stay of these 20 cases pending an appeal of the acquittal of the defendants in the criminal trial. The judge was scheduled to deliver his judgment on the motion to stay in February 2017.

Independent Monitoring: The government continued to grant local and international NGOs access to prisons and prisoners but required them to obtain permission from the commissioner general of prisons. The International Committee of the Red Cross (ICRC) continued to visit detainees of the Caprivi treason trial in both Windhoek Central Prison and Oluno Prison, and helped arrange for family visits. Staff from the UN High Commissioner for Refugees (UNHCR) visited incarcerated refugees and asylum seekers charged with crimes.

Improvements: During the year police continued to improve detention conditions by refurbishing older facilities and by building additional holding cells.

d. Arbitrary Arrest or Detention

The constitution and law prohibit arbitrary arrest or detention, and the government generally observed these prohibitions.

Role of the Police and Security Apparatus

The Namibian Police Force (NamPol) has approximately 16,500 uniformed officers and operates under the Ministry of Safety and Security. The Namibian Defense Force, with an estimated 17,500 active duty members, is part of the Ministry of Defense. NamPol is responsible for internal security, while the defense force provides supplemental assistance in response to some natural disasters.

NamPol reported it had decentralized policing activities to make regional commands responsible for executing directives of the inspector general of police. Authorities assigned approximately half of NamPol's personnel to the Special Field Force responsible for guard duty, checkpoints, and the maintenance of public order. Civilian authorities maintained effective control over NamPol, and the government had effective mechanisms to investigate and punish abuse and corruption. There were cases of police corruption and impunity. According to NamPol, from April 2014 to March 2015, authorities opened 215 cases involving complaints against police officers and suspended 40 officers. While NamPol generally lacked the resources, training, and personnel to deter or investigate street crime effectively, it continued to increase street patrols, community policing, and programs involving community volunteers to address the problems.

Police continued to receive human rights training from various sources. NamPol continued to maintain a legal office to conduct internal training. It trained police on the requirement to bring arrested persons before a magistrate within 48 hours of arrest and on the legal requirements for police searches. The Ombudsman's Office completed antitorture training begun in 2015. NamPol continued to operate a Women's Network to advocate for equality of and equity for female police officers.

Arrest Procedures and Treatment of Detainees

Arrest warrants are not required in all cases, including when authorities apprehend a suspect in the course of committing a crime. Authorities must inform persons arrested of the reason for their arrest, and police generally informed detainees promptly of the charges against them. Authorities must arraign arrested persons within 48 hours of their detention. The government did not always meet this requirement, especially in rural areas far from courts. The constitution stipulates the accused are entitled to defense by legal counsel of their choice, and authorities respected this right.

The state-funded Legal Aid Directorate (LAD) provided free legal assistance for indigent defendants in criminal cases and, depending on resource availability, in civil matters. The LAD provided assistance in approximately 70 percent of all criminal cases.

There was a functioning bail system. Officials generally allowed detainees prompt access to family members. The constitution permits detention without trial during a state of emergency but requires publication of the names of detainees in the government's gazette within 14 days of their apprehension. An advisory board appointed by the president on the recommendation of the Judicial Service Commission (the constitutional body that recommends judges to the president for appointment) must review their cases within one month of detention and every three months thereafter. The constitution requires such advisory boards to not have more than five members of which at least three must be "Judges of the Supreme Court or the High Court or qualified to be such." The advisory board has the power to order the release of anyone detained without trial during an emergency.

Pretrial Detention: Lengthy pretrial detention remained a significant problem. A shortage of qualified magistrates and other court officials, the cost to the government of providing legal aid, slow or incomplete police investigations, and procedural postponements resulted in a serious backlog of criminal cases. Delays between arrest and trial could last for years. There were lengthy delays in criminal appeals as well. A 2003 appeal of a murder conviction was heard in 2004, but the court did not render its decision until December 2015 after the man had served his sentence and been released. To relieve court backlogs, two courthouse construction or renovation projects continued.

Detainee's Ability to Challenge Lawfulness of Detention before a Court: Persons arrested or detained are entitled to challenge in court the legal basis or arbitrary nature of their detention and obtain prompt release and compensation if found to have been unlawfully detained.

e. Denial of Fair Public Trial

The constitution provides for an independent judiciary, and the courts acted independently at times, making judgments and rulings critical of the government. Inefficiency and lack of resources, however, hampered the judicial system.

Customary courts hear many civil and petty criminal cases in rural areas. The law delineates the offenses the customary system may handle. Customary courts deal with infractions of local customary law among members of the same ethnic group. The law defines the role, duties, and powers of traditional leaders and states customary law inconsistent with the constitution is invalid. Cases resolved in customary courts were sometimes tried a second time in government courts.

Trial Procedures

The constitution and law provide for the right to a fair public trial, but long delays in courts hearing cases and the uneven application of constitutional protections in the customary system compromised this right. The backlog of criminal cases awaiting trial increased from 1,344 in 2011 to 10,544 in September 2015. Defendants are presumed innocent. The law provides for defendants to be informed promptly and in detail of the charges against them, in a language they understand, and of their right to a public trial.

All defendants have the right to be present at trial, to consult with an attorney in a timely manner, and--with their attorney--to have access to government-held evidence. Defendants receive free interpretation as necessary from their first court appearance through all appeals. Although indigent defendants are entitled to a lawyer provided by the state in criminal and civil cases, this sometimes did not occur due to an insufficient number of public defenders, insufficient state funds to pay private lawyers to represent indigent defendants, or because the LAD did not accept the application for representation from an accused.

Defendants may confront witnesses, present witnesses and evidence on their behalf, and have the right of appeal. The law extends these rights to all citizens. The courts provided defendants adequate time and facilities to prepare their defense. Defendants have the right not to testify against themselves or confess guilt.

In 1999 separatists attacked government facilities and buildings in Katima Mulilo, the largest city of Caprivi Region (renamed Zambezi Region in 2013). A trial originally involving 131 defendants alleged to have participated in the attacks began in 2003 and concluded in 2015. In October the prosecutor general requested leave to appeal the acquittal of 41 of the defendants. Further hearings on the request were scheduled for March 2017.

In 2014 the Supreme Court overturned the 2007 convictions of nine other defendants. The court ordered they be retried. Following the start of the retrial, eight of the defendants challenged the trial court's jurisdiction, arguing their deportation from Botswana and handover to the custody of Namibian authorities violated international law. In August the Supreme Court ruled only one of the eight defendants was illegally handed over to Namibian authorities in Botswana and ordered all charges against him dropped. The retrial of the other seven and the defendant who had not challenged jurisdiction continued at year's end.

The separate trial of Albius Moto Liseli, whose 2009 arrest made him the last person arrested in connection with the plot, continued during the year.

Political Prisoners and Detainees

There were no reports of political prisoners or detainees.

Civil Judicial Procedures and Remedies

The law provides for access to a court to file lawsuits seeking damages for or cessation of human rights violations. The constitution provides for administrative procedures to correct, as well as judicial remedies to redress, wrongs. Civil court orders were mostly well enforced.

Most of the Caprivi defendants filed civil suits at different points during incarceration starting as early as 2001, alleging unlawful arrest, torture at the time of their arrests, and excessive time in jail awaiting trial. The LAC represented many of the defendants and settled the remaining civil cases by the end of 2015. Civil lawsuits filed by nine acquitted defendants began in November. The civil cases of 20 other acquitted defendants were also pending at year's end.

f. Arbitrary or Unlawful Interference with Privacy, Family, Home, or Correspondence

The constitution prohibits such actions, and there were no reports the government failed to respect these prohibitions.

Section 2. Respect for Civil Liberties, Including:

a. Freedom of Speech and Press

The constitution provides for freedom of speech and press, and the government generally respected these rights. An independent press, an effective judiciary, and a functioning democratic political system combined to promote freedom of speech and press. Government and party leaders, however, at times criticized the press.

<u>Press and Media Freedoms</u>: Independent media were active and expressed a wide variety of views without restriction.

<u>Violence and Harassment</u>: On April 15, authorities detained and questioned two journalists working for a Japanese television station investigating ties between the Democratic People's Republic of Korea (DPRK) and Namibia at Hosea Kutako International Airport outside Windhoek. Authorities released them after searching their luggage and confiscating two laptops and three cameras. The journalists claimed they were detained because Netumbo Nandi-Ndaitwah, deputy prime minister and minister of international relations and cooperation, was upset by questions they asked during an interview with her a few hours earlier. The journalists were allowed to depart the country the same day. On April 19, a police spokesperson was quoted in media as justifying the temporary detention of the two journalists and the confiscation of their equipment because the journalists "might have captured material that could hamper national safety." In an April 20 speech in parliament, Tjekero Tweya, minister of information and communication technology, alleged the journalists misused their filming permit by invading the privacy of showering North Korean construction workers at a military base. Tweya also said the journalists "compromised the security of a sovereign state." Authorities eventually returned the journalists' confiscated equipment to the Japanese embassy in Windhoek.

<u>Censorship or Content Restrictions</u>: There were reports journalists working for state-owned media practiced self-censorship in favor of the government and Swapo.

Internet Freedom

The government did not restrict or disrupt access to the internet or censor online content, and there were no credible reports the government monitored private online communication without appropriate legal authority. The law allows the intelligence services to monitor e-mails and internet usage with authorization from any magistrate. According to the International Telecommunication Union, 22.31 percent of individuals used the internet in 2015, while a 2014 study by the Ministry of Information and Communication Technology found the rate of internet usage was 40 percent. The discrepancy may be due to the latter taking greater account of internet usage from mobile platforms.

Academic Freedom and Cultural Events

Regulations published in 2013 make it illegal to conduct research in the country--whether publicly or privately funded--without authorization from the government-appointed National Commission on Research, Science, and Technology. The regulation defines "research" so broadly it could be construed to cover investigative work by lawyers, doctors, journalists, and students. Conviction of violations of the regulations is punishable by five years' imprisonment or fines of N$20,000 ($1,440) and an indefinite ban on conducting research in the country. In March 2015 the LAC filed a constitutional challenge to the regulations. The challenge was scheduled for consideration in January 2017.

b. Freedom of Peaceful Assembly and Association

The constitution and law provide for the freedoms of assembly and association, and the government generally respected these rights. Government institutions of higher learning, including the University of Namibia and the Namibian University of Science and Technology, however, continued to ban activities by political organizations on campus.

c. Freedom of Religion

See the Department of State's *International Religious Freedom Report* at www.state.gov/religiousfreedomreport/.

d. Freedom of Movement, Internally Displaced Persons, Protection of Refugees, and Stateless Persons

The constitution and law provide for freedom of internal movement, foreign travel, emigration, and repatriation, and the government generally respected these rights.

Abuse of Migrants, Refugees, and Stateless Persons: The government cooperated with UNHCR and other humanitarian organizations in providing protection and assistance to internally displaced persons (IDPs), refugees, returning refugees, asylum seekers, stateless persons, or other persons of concern.

Protection of Refugees

<u>Access to Asylum</u>: The law provides for the granting of asylum or refugee status, and the government has an established system for providing protection to refugees.

Refugees were required to live at the government's Osire refugee settlement. The government cooperated with the NGO Africa Humanitarian Action to provide food, shelter, water, and sanitation at the settlement. The government continued to issue identification cards and exit permits allowing refugees to leave the settlement to travel to a specified place for a limited period. The government maintained strict control over civilian access to the Osire refugee settlement but provided regular unrestricted access to the ICRC, UNHCR, and UNHCR's NGO partners.

<u>Refoulement</u>: In 2015 UNHCR received a report authorities denied asylum to three male applicants from Burundi and sent them back to Burundi. UNHCR negotiated with the government for their return, but there was no resolution by year's end.

<u>Employment</u>: The government maintained restrictive measures on refugees' ability to work, stating it was seeking to protect the jobs of citizens. Refugees wishing to work outside Osire Camp were required to seek government permission and work permits.

<u>Durable Solutions</u>: Between 2014 and 2015, the government issued permanent residence permits to 123 of 476 former refugee families that were unwilling to repatriate to Angola. UNHCR paid the fees associated with the permits and requested the government waive fees for the remaining families, but at year's end the permits had yet to be issued.

Section 3. Freedom to Participate in the Political Process

The constitution and law provide citizens the ability to choose their government in free and fair periodic elections held by secret ballot and based on universal and equal suffrage.

Elections and Political Participation

<u>Recent Elections</u>: In the November 2015 regional and local council elections, the ruling Swapo party won 112 of 121 regional council seats and gained control of 54 of 57 local districts. Voting proceeded in an orderly and effective manner with no reports of politically motivated violence or voter intimidation. In the 2014 presidential and parliamentary elections, voters elected Swapo candidate Hage

Geingob president with 87 percent of the vote. Swapo candidates won 77 of the 96 elected seats (there are also eight appointed seats) in the National Assembly, the lower house of parliament. International observers characterized the elections in 2014 and 2015 as generally free and fair.

Participation of Women and Minorities: Virtually all of the country's ethnic minorities had representatives in parliament and in senior positions in the cabinet. The president is from the minority Damara ethnic group. Historic economic and educational disadvantages, however, continued to limit the participation in politics of some ethnic groups, such as the San and Himba.

Section 4. Corruption and Lack of Transparency in Government

The law provides criminal penalties for corruption by officials; however, the government did not implement the law effectively, and officials sometimes engaged in corrupt practices with impunity. There were isolated reports of corruption by individuals in government. During the year the Anti-Corruption Commission (ACC) continued awareness campaigns and workshops for government officials, politicians, civil society organizations, church leaders, and schoolchildren on the dangers of corruption.

Corruption: The ACC, Prosecutor General's Office, NamPol, Auditor General's Office, Financial Investigative Center at the Bank of Namibia, Public Service Commission, and Ombudsman's Office are responsible for combating corruption. The ACC receives and investigates corruption complaints, often from the public. The Financial Investigative Center investigates and reports suspicious money transfers. The Public Service Commission investigates corruption complaints in the civil service hiring process. The Auditor General's Office also investigates corruption and refers cases to the Prosecutor General's Office and NamPol for further investigation and criminal prosecution where appropriate. These organizations actively collaborated with civil society, conducted thorough investigations, and operated both effectively and independently.

Financial Disclosure: In October 2015 the National Assembly adopted a parliamentary code of conduct requiring the annual declaration of financial interests. The adopted declaration form included a confidential portion to which the public does not have access. In May 2015 the president voluntarily published an accounting of his and his wife's assets. As of August, 85 of the 104 members of the National Assembly had declared their assets. On July 14, Minister of Finance Calle Schlettwein voluntarily and publicly declared his assets. The National

Council, the country's upper house of parliament, released an annual register listing its members' financial interests.

<u>Public Access to Information</u>: The law prohibits public employees from sharing information held by a government ministry without permission from the minister or permanent secretary of the ministry. No law provides for public access to government information, but media outlets generally found the government willing to provide information when requested.

Section 5. Governmental Attitude Regarding International and Nongovernmental Investigation of Alleged Violations of Human Rights

A number of domestic and international human rights groups generally operated without government restriction, investigating and publishing their findings on human rights cases. Government officials were somewhat cooperative and responsive to their views. The Ombudsman's Office, local human rights NGOs, and the ACC reported NamPol cooperated and assisted in corruption and human rights investigations.

<u>Government Human Rights Bodies</u>: There is an autonomous ombudsman with whom other government agencies cooperated. Observers considered him effective in addressing some corruption and human rights problems. Between January and September 9, the Ombudsman's Office reported 226 human rights-related complaints, 70 of which it deemed to be supported by the facts and 74 not supported by the facts. As of September 9, 82 cases remained undecided.

Section 6. Discrimination, Societal Abuses, and Trafficking in Persons

Women

<u>Rape and Domestic Violence</u>: The law defines rape in broad terms and allows for the prosecution of spousal rape. The courts tried numerous cases of rape during the year, and the government generally enforced court sentences providing between five and 45 years' imprisonment for those convicted. Between January and July 2015, police received reports of 565 rapes. Women's groups and NGOs believed the actual prevalence of rape was higher, with only a small fraction of cases prosecuted and fewer still resulting in conviction. Factors hampering rape prosecutions included limited police capacity and the withdrawal of allegations by alleged victims after the filing of charges, often because the victims either receive

compensation from the accused; succumb to family pressure, shame, or threats; or become discouraged at the length of time involved in prosecuting a case.

Traditional authorities may adjudicate civil claims for compensation in cases of rape, but criminal trials for rape are held in criminal courts.

The government and media focused national attention on gender-based violence (GBV). Between January and August 2015, police reported 39 GBV cases resulting in death. The president and former presidents spoke publicly against GBV.

The law prohibits domestic violence, but the problem was widespread. Penalties for conviction of domestic violence--including physical abuse, sexual abuse, economic abuse, intimidation, harassment, and serious emotional, verbal, or psychological abuse--range from a fine of N$300 ($21) for simple offenses to 10 years' imprisonment and a fine for assault with intent to cause grievous bodily harm.

The law provides for the issuance of protection orders in cases of domestic violence and specifies that certain crimes of violence--including murder, rape, and assault--be handled differently if the crimes take place within a domestic relationship. When authorities received reports of domestic violence, Gender-based Violence Protection Units intervened.

There were 15 Gender-based Violence Protection Units (formerly called women and child protection units) staffed with police officers, social workers, legal advisors, and medical personnel trained to assist victims of sexual assault. The Ministries of Justice, Health and Social Services, and Gender Equality and Child Welfare, along with NGOs, provided training to some members of these units. Some magistrate courts provided special courtrooms with a cubicle constructed of one-way glass and child-friendly waiting rooms to protect vulnerable witnesses from open testimony. A privately run shelter for victims of GBV violence in the Khomas region operated effectively. The Ministry of Gender Equality and Child Welfare owned shelters in the other regions. Due to staffing and funding shortfalls, however, the shelters housing victims operated only on an as-needed basis with social workers coordinating with volunteers to place victims in shelters and assist them with food and other services.

Sexual Harassment: The law explicitly prohibits sexual harassment in the workplace. Employees who leave their jobs due to sexual harassment may be entitled to legal "remedies available to an employee who has been unfairly dismissed." Employees rarely filed sexual harassment claims, and thus the law against sexual harassment was not frequently enforced.

Reproductive Rights: Couples and individuals have the right to decide the number, spacing, and timing of their children; manage their reproductive health; and have access to the information and means to do so, free from discrimination, coercion, or violence. There are no government restrictions on the provision of contraceptives except to children under age 14, the legal age of consent for medical treatment (parental consent would be required for a younger child), and 50 percent of women used a modern contraceptive method. Women who lived in urban areas had better access to skilled attendance during childbirth and postpartum care than those in rural areas. The country's *2014 Demographic and Health Survey* reported the 2013 maternal mortality ratio was 385 per 100,000 live births. General lack of access to effective health care in treating eclampsia, hemorrhage, and obstructed or prolonged labor contributed to maternal mortality. HIV/AIDS was the leading indirect cause of maternal mortality, linked to almost 4.3 percent of maternal deaths.

Discrimination: The law prohibits gender-based discrimination, including employment discrimination. Women nonetheless experienced discrimination in such areas as access to credit, salary level, owning and managing businesses, education, and housing (see section 7.d.). The law prohibits discriminatory practices against women married under civil law, but women married under customary law face legal and cultural discrimination. The constitution forbids discrimination on the basis of gender, and the law generally provides for the same legal status and rights for women as for men, with three exceptions: firstly, some elements of customary family law provide for different treatment of women, such as providing different grounds for divorce and different divorce procedures; secondly, the law governing marital property is based solely on the domicile of the husband at the time of the marriage; and thirdly, the law grants maternity leave to mothers but not paternity leave to fathers. The law protects a widow's right to remain on the land of her deceased husband, even if she remarries. Traditional practices in certain northern regions, however, continued to permit family members to confiscate the property of deceased men from their widows and children; NGOs and activists continued to work to decrease the prevalence of this practice. The Ministry of Gender Equality and Child Welfare is responsible for advocating for women's rights.

Children

<u>Birth Registration</u>: The constitution provides for citizenship by birth within the country to a citizen parent or a foreign parent ordinarily resident in the country, or to those born outside the country to citizen parents. A June 23 Supreme Court decision interpreted the meaning of the phrase "ordinarily resident" more broadly than the government's preferred interpretation and ordered the government to issue a birth certificate to the child of Dutch parents living in the country on work permits. In response the government sought parliamentary approval of a bill forbidding issuance of the child's birth certificate and imposing an interpretation of "ordinarily resident" that differed from the Supreme Court's interpretation. In early August, in the face of public opposition and rejection of the bill by the National Council, the government dropped its opposition to the court decision and announced it would issue a birth certificate to the child.

According to the Ministry of Home Affairs and Immigration, approximately 98 percent of citizens had a birth certificate or other identifying document. Parents who did not register their children at birth often faced a lengthy registration process.

The Ministry of Home Affairs and Immigration, in partnership with the UN Children's Fund, continued efforts to provide birth certificates for newborns at clinics and hospitals throughout the country, including through mobile registration vans and birth registration offices at 11 high-volume hospitals.

<u>Child Abuse</u>: Child abuse was a serious problem, and authorities prosecuted reported crimes against children, particularly rape and incest. One-third of reported rapes involved child victims. In 2012 (the latest year for which statistics were available) approximately 870 children and juveniles were reported killed, raped, or assaulted. Police reported six cases of incest perpetrated on children between January and July 2015. NGOs believed the true incidence of child abuse greatly exceeded the number of reported cases. The Ministry of Gender Equality and Child Welfare employed social workers throughout the country to address cases of child abuse, and conducted public awareness campaigns aimed at preventing child abuse and publicizing services available to victims. The Ombudsman's Office also continued a public campaign to educate children about their rights.

<u>Early and Forced Marriage</u>: The law prohibits civil marriages before age 18 for both boys and girls. The Child Care and Protection Act prohibits customary marriage before age 18.

<u>Sexual Exploitation of Children</u>: The law criminalizes child pornography, child prostitution, and the actions of both the client and the pimp in cases of sexual exploitation of children under age 18, but sexual exploitation of children occurred. NGOs that worked with persons in prostitution reported that in most cases children engaged in prostitution without third-party involvement due to economic pressures or as a means of survival among HIV/AIDS orphans and other vulnerable children. A 2013 study at a nonprofit center to assist persons in prostitution in Windhoek found the average age at which women at the center entered into prostitution was 15.4 years.

The penalties for conviction of soliciting a child under age 16 for sex, or more generally for commercial sexual exploitation of a child (including through pornography), is a fine of up to N$40,000 ($2,800), up to 10 years' imprisonment, or both. Exposing a child to pornography is also illegal. Penalties for conviction in cases involving children ages 16 and 17 are the same as for adults. The law makes special provisions to protect vulnerable witnesses, including individuals under age 18 or against whom a sexual offense has been committed.

An adult convicted of engaging in sexual relations with a child in prostitution under age 16 may be imprisoned for up to 15 years for a first offense and up to 45 years for a repeat offense. Any person who aids and abets trafficking in persons-- including child prostitution--within the country or across the border is liable to a fine of up to one million Namibian dollars ($70,000) or imprisonment for up to 50 years. Conviction of solicitation of a prostitute, living off the earnings of prostitution, or keeping a brothel carries penalties of N$40,000 ($2,800), 10 years' imprisonment, or both.

The minimum legal age for consensual sex is 16. The penalty for conviction of statutory rape--sex with a child under age 14 when the perpetrator is more than three years older than the victim--is a minimum of 15 years in prison when the victim is under 13 and a minimum of five years when the victim is 13. There is no minimum penalty for conviction of sexual relations with a child between ages 14 and 16. Possession of or trade in child pornography is illegal. The government continued to train police officials in handling of child sex abuse cases. Centers for abused women and children worked to reduce the trauma suffered by abused children.

HIV/AIDS orphans (whose numbers declined during the year) remained vulnerable to sexual abuse and exploitation.

<u>Infanticide or Infanticide of Children with Disabilities</u>: The media continued to report cases in which parents, usually young mothers, abandoned newborns, sometimes leading to the newborns' death. The government enforced prohibitions against this practice by investigating and prosecuting violators.

<u>International Child Abductions</u>: The country is not a party to the 1980 Hague Convention on the Civil Aspects of International Child abduction. See the Department of State's *Annual Report on International Parental Child Abduction* at travel.state.gov/content/childabduction/en/legal/compliance,html.

Anti-Semitism

There was a Jewish community of approximately 100 individuals, the majority of whose members lived in Windhoek. There were no reports of anti-Semitic acts.

Trafficking in Persons

See the Department of State's *Trafficking in Persons Report* at www.state.gov/j/tip/rls/tiprpt/.

Persons with Disabilities

The constitution protects the rights of "all members of the human family," which domestic legal experts understand to prohibit discrimination against persons with disabilities. The law prohibits discrimination against persons with physical and mental disabilities in employment, health care, education, or the provision of other state services. The law prohibits discrimination in any employment decision based on a number of factors, including any "degree of physical or mental disability" (see section 7.d.). It makes an exception in the case of a person with a disability if that person is, because of disability, unable to perform the duties or functions of the job in question. Enforcement in this area was ineffective, and societal discrimination persisted.

The government requires all newly constructed government buildings be accessible and include ramps and other features facilitating access. The government, however, neither mandates access to already constructed public buildings generally nor requires retrofitting of government buildings.

Children with disabilities attended mainstream schools. The law does not restrict the rights of persons with disabilities to vote and otherwise participate in civic affairs, but infrastructure challenges at public venues hindered the ability of persons with disabilities to participate in civic life.

A deputy minister of disability affairs in the office of the vice president is responsible for matters related to persons with disabilities, including operation of the National Disability Council of Namibia. The council is responsible for overseeing concerns of persons with disabilities and coordinating implementation of policies on persons with disabilities with government ministries and agencies.

National/Racial/Ethnic Minorities

Despite constitutional prohibitions, societal, racial, and ethnic discrimination persisted.

Indigenous People

Other ethnic groups have historically exploited the San, the country's earliest known inhabitants. By law all traditional communities, including the San, participate without discrimination in decisions affecting their lands, cultures, traditions, and allocation of natural resources. The San, however, were unable to exercise these rights fully because of minimal access to education, limited economic opportunities, and their relative isolation. Teachers and nurses, when available, often did not speak any of the San languages. Some San had difficulty obtaining a government identification card because they lacked birth certificates or other identification. Without a government-issued identification card, the San could not access government social programs or register to vote. A lack of police presence and courts prevented San women from reporting and seeking protection from GBV.

Indigenous lands were effectively demarcated but poorly managed. Many San tribes lived on conservancy (communal) lands but were unable to prevent the surrounding larger ethnic groups from using and exploiting those lands. Some San claimed regional officials refused to remove other ethnic groups from San lands.

Human rights NGOs, such as the Namibia San Council, Working Group of Indigenous Minorities in Southern Africa, LAC, and NamRights, helped San communities assert their basic human rights during the year.

Acts of Violence, Discrimination, and Other Abuses Based on Sexual Orientation and Gender Identity

Although laws inherited at independence criminalize sodomy, the ban was not enforced. The law defines sodomy as intentional anal sexual relations between men. This definition excludes anal sexual relations between heterosexual couples and sexual relations between lesbians. Many citizens considered all same-sex sexual activity taboo, however. The prohibition against sexual discrimination in the constitution did not prohibit discrimination based on sexual orientation.

LGBTI (lesbian, gay, bisexual, transgender, and intersex) persons continued to face harassment when trying to access public services. Some politicians opposed any legislation that would specifically protect the rights of lesbian, gay, bisexual, transgender, and intersex persons. On August 23, the ombudsman publicly declared his support for the legalization of same-sex marriage and the abolition of the common law offense of sodomy.

HIV and AIDS Social Stigma

Societal discrimination against and stigmatization of persons with HIV/AIDS remained problems.

Potential military recruits were tested for HIV, and those found positive were unable to join, but persons who test positive for HIV while in the service received treatment and were allowed to stay in the military. Applicants seeking to join the police were tested for HIV. Those testing positive were given a second test to assess the progression of the disease, and candidates found to have healthy CD4 (white blood cell) counts were allowed to join. NamPol had HIV-positive officers on its force. Some jobs in the civilian sector require a pre-employment test for HIV, but there were no reports of employment discrimination specifically based on HIV/AIDS status.

Section 7. Worker Rights

a. Freedom of Association and the Right to Collective Bargaining

The law provides for the right to form and join independent unions, conduct legal strikes, and bargain collectively; however, the law prohibits workers in "essential services" such as the police, military, and correctional facilities from joining unions. No legal provision provides for the right of trade unions or federations of trade unions to establish or join confederations.

Except for workers in public health, safety, and other essential services, workers may strike once mandatory conciliation procedures are exhausted and 48 hours' notice is given to the employer and labor commissioner. Workers may take strike actions only in disputes involving specific worker interests, such as pay raises.

Disputes over worker rights, including dismissals, must first be submitted to conciliation and then are referred to a labor court for arbitration if conciliation is unsuccessful. The law provides for conciliation and arbitration to resolve labor disputes more quickly, although employers and unions publicly questioned the system's effectiveness. The law prohibits unfair dismissal of workers engaged in legal strikes, specifically prohibits employer retaliation against both union organizers and striking workers, and provides for reinstatement for workers dismissed for union activity so long as the workers' actions at the time were not in violation of other laws.

The law provides employees with the right to bargain individually or collectively and for recognition of the exclusive collective bargaining power of a union when a majority of the workers are members of that union. The law provides for the protection of all workers, including migrants, nonessential public sector workers, domestic workers, and those in export processing zones.

The government generally enforced the law on collective bargaining but not always effectively. The Ministry of Labor, Industrial Relations, and Employment Creation continued to cite lack of information and basic negotiation skills as factors hampering workers' ability to bargain with employers successfully.

In general the government and employers respected freedom of association and workers exercised this right. The government effectively enforced applicable laws on freedom of association. Many trade unions officially affiliated with the Swapo party, which many workers argued limited their independence in promoting worker rights. Aside from mediation efforts, the government was not directly involved in union activities. Employers also did not appear to interfere in union activities.

Farm workers and domestic servants working on rural and remote farms often did not know their rights. When attempting to organize these workers, unions experienced obstacles such as prohibitions from entering commercial farms. Some activists alleged political interference in rural areas as well. As a result some farm workers reportedly suffered abuse by employers, including poor access to health care.

Workers exercised their right to strike in the education, mining, and fishing sectors. The majority of strikes involved allegations of unfair dismissal, as well as demands for higher pay, more benefits, or improved working conditions. The most serious strike involved fisheries workers and began in October 2015. As of September the strike continued. Because the striking workers were members of an unrecognized union, the strike was declared illegal. More than 1,000 workers claimed they were unfairly dismissed because of their participation in the strike. As of September the government continued negotiations with the teachers union to prevent a pending nationwide strike regarding wages.

Collective bargaining was not practiced widely outside the mining, construction, agriculture, and public service sectors. Almost all collective bargaining was at the workplace and company level. Employers respected the collective bargaining process.

The law requires employers to provide equal labor rights to all their employees. Employers may apply to the minister of labor and social services for an exemption from these provisions if they can prove workers' rights are protected, but very few employers pursued this option.

b. Prohibition of Forced or Compulsory Labor

The law prohibits all forms of forced or compulsory labor, including by children. Persons convicted of forced or compulsory labor face a maximum fine of N$20,000 ($1,400), four years' imprisonment, or both. The government did not effectively enforce the law. The government did not report any formal allegations of forced or compulsory labor; it investigated child labor when reported. Resources, inspections, and remediation were inadequate. Penalties for violations were insufficient to deter violations.

Also see the Department of State's *Trafficking in Persons Report* at www.state.gov/j/tip/rls/tiprpt/.

c. Prohibition of Child Labor and Minimum Age for Employment

The minimum age for employment is 14, with higher age requirements for night work and in certain sectors such as mining and construction. Children under age

16 may not engage in hazardous work, including working between the hours of 8 p.m. and 7 a.m., underground work, mining, construction work, or in facilities where goods are manufactured or electricity is generated, transformed, or distributed, or machinery is installed or dismantled. Children ages 16 and 17 may perform hazardous work subject to approval by the Ministry of Labor, Industrial Relations and Employment Creation and restrictions outlined in the Labor Act. Persons convicted of employing children face a maximum fine of N$20,000 ($1,400), four years' imprisonment, or both. The Child Care and Protection Act also includes provisions prohibiting child labor.

Gender-based Violence Protection Units enforced child labor laws in cooperation with the Ministry of Labor, Industrial Relations, and Employment Creation. The ministry made special provisions in its labor inspections to look for underage workers and it prioritized such investigations, often targeting smaller towns and districts. The government trained all inspectors to identify the worst forms of child labor. Small-scale labor inspections continued on a regular basis.

The ministry conducted programs aimed at encouraging parents and guardians to allow children to attend school. It also operated a program in Windhoek to arrange housing and school enrollment for homeless children. Primary and secondary school education was free, and the government provided free school stationery during the year.

The Ministry of Gender Equality and Child Welfare and the Ministry of Health and Social Services coordinated welfare programs for orphans, including those affected by HIV/AIDS, through grants and scholarships to keep them in school. In partnership with the International Labor Organization, the government also participated in a four-year program to withdraw children from and prevent them from entering exploitive labor in agriculture and adult-coerced criminal activity. The government continued to distribute a comprehensive guide on the labor law that included a section on child labor. The government also worked with NGOs, such as Project Hope, to assist victims of child labor.

Child labor continued to be a problem, however. The UN Children's Fund reported that in 2011 (the latest year for which statistics were available) child labor rates were 3.9 percent for rural children ages 10 to 14 and 2.6 percent for children ages eight to 11. Children worked mostly on communal farms owned by their families herding cattle, goats, and sheep. Children also worked as child minders or domestic servants and in family businesses.

Also see the Department of Labor's *Findings on the Worst Forms of Child Labor* at www.dol.gov/ilab/reports/child-labor/findings/.

d. Discrimination with Respect to Employment and Occupation

The labor law prohibits discrimination in employment and occupation based on race, sex, religion, political opinion, national origin or citizenship, pregnancy, family responsibility, disability, age, language, social status, and HIV-positive status, and the government in general effectively enforced the law. The law requires equal pay for equal work. The law does not specifically address employment discrimination based on sexual or gender orientation.

Migrant workers enjoy the same legal protections, wages, and working conditions as citizens.

The Ministry of Labor, Industrial Relations and Employment Creation and the Employment Equity Commission both report to the minister of labor and are responsible for addressing complaints of discrimination in employment. The minimum penalties for violation of antidiscrimination provisions are N$4,000 ($280) or two years' imprisonment; the maximum penalties are N$100,000 ($7,000), five years' imprisonment, or both. Penalties were sufficient to deter violations, and the government prosecuted businesses accused of violating antidiscrimination laws.

Discrimination in employment and occupation occurred with respect to gender (see section 6) and race, most frequently in the mining and construction industries. Men occupied approximately two-thirds of upper management positions in both the private and public sectors.

e. Acceptable Conditions of Work

There was no generally applicable minimum wage law. In 2015 the government established a minimum wage for domestic workers of N$1,218 ($85) per month and provided for it to increase annually at the rate of the consumer price index plus 5 percent. The mining, construction, security, and agricultural sectors set basic levels of pay in each of their sectors through collective bargaining. In the latest comparative analysis in *Namibia Household Income and Expenditure Surveys* (NHIES), the Namibia Statistics Agency reported that in 2009-10 citizens were considered "poor" if they earned less than N$378 ($26) per month and "severely poor" if they earned less than N$278 ($19) per month; 29 percent of citizens lived below the poverty line, and 16 percent of the population was extremely poor.

The standard legal workweek was 45 hours, with at least 36 consecutive hours of rest between workweeks. By law an employer may not require more than 10 hours' overtime work per week and must pay premium pay for overtime work. The law mandates 20 workdays of annual leave per year for those working a five-day workweek and 24 workdays of annual leave per year for those working a six-day workweek. The law also requires employees receive paid time off for government holidays, receive five days of compassionate leave per year, at least 30 workdays of sick leave during a three-year period, and three months of maternity leave paid by the employer and the Social Security Commission.

The Ministry of Labor, Industrial Relations, and Employment Creation mandates occupational safety and health standards, and the law empowers the authorities to enforce these standards through inspections and criminal penalties. The law requires employers to provide for the health, safety, and welfare of their employees. The law covers all employers and employees in the country including individuals placed by a private employment agency (labor hire), except independent contractors and members of the National Defense Force, Namibian Intelligence Service, the Prison Service, and the police.

The government did not always enforce labor laws effectively. As of October 4, there were 97 labor inspectors, which was insufficient to address violations. Inspections occurred proactively, reactively, and at random. In view of the ministry's resource constraints in vehicles, budget, and personnel, as well as difficulty in gaining access to some large communal and commercial farms and private households, labor inspectors sometimes found it difficult to investigate possible violations. The Ministry of Labor, Industrial Relations, and Employment Creation established a national task force on safety but lacked resources to monitor adherence, especially in small family-owned operations. The law provides that persons convicted of violating safety regulations face a maximum fine of N$2,000 ($140), six months' imprisonment, or both; however, the penalties were insufficient to deter violations, and labor law violations occurred.

The Namibian Employers' Federation reported most prominent offenses concerning employee rights and working conditions were in the informal sector, including the common informal bars known as "shebeens." Most offenders were Chinese owners of retail shops, who underpaid and overworked their employees.

Allegations persisted that, apart from failing to adhere to the labor code concerning hiring and firing, Chinese firms failed to pay sectorally established minimum wages and benefits in certain industries, failed to respect workhour regulations for public holidays and Sundays, and ignored occupational health and safety measures; for example, requiring construction workers to sleep on site.

Migrant workers have the same legal rights as citizens.

By law employees have the right to remove themselves from dangerous work situations, and authorities effectively protected employees in this situation.